READING/WRITING COMPANION

Mc
Graw
Hill
Education

Cover: Nathan Love, Erwin Madrid

mheducation.com/prek-12

Send all inquiries to:
McGraw-Hill Education
Two Penn Plaza
New York, NY 10121

ISBN: 978-0-07-901807-6
MHID: 0-07-901807-6

Printed in the United States of America.

7 8 9 LMN 23 22 21   C

Welcome to Wonders!

Read exciting **Literature**, **Science**, and **Social Studies** texts!

★ **LEARN** about the world around you!

★ **THINK**, **SPEAK**, and **WRITE** about genres!

★ **COLLABORATE** in discussion and inquiry!

★ **EXPRESS** yourself!

my.mheducation.com
Use your student login to read core texts, practice grammar and spelling, explore research projects and more!

GENRE STUDY 1 EXPOSITORY TEXT

Lisa Thornberg/E+/Getty Images

GENRE STUDY 2 FABLE

Peter Francis

GENRE STUDY 3 POETRY

WRAP UP THE UNIT

SCIENCE

Talk About It

This baby penguin and mother look different, but they are the same in many ways. They both have layers of fat to keep warm. They are both birds, not mammals. They both use their flippers to swim.

Talk with a partner about how baby penguins are the same and different from their parents. Speak clearly at a pace that makes sense. Write your ideas on the chart.

Same	Different

TAKE NOTES

Knowing why you are reading a text can help you pay attention to important details. Write a purpose for reading the expository text here.

_____

_____

_____

_____

As you read, make note of:

Interesting Words _____

_____

Key Details _____

_____

_____

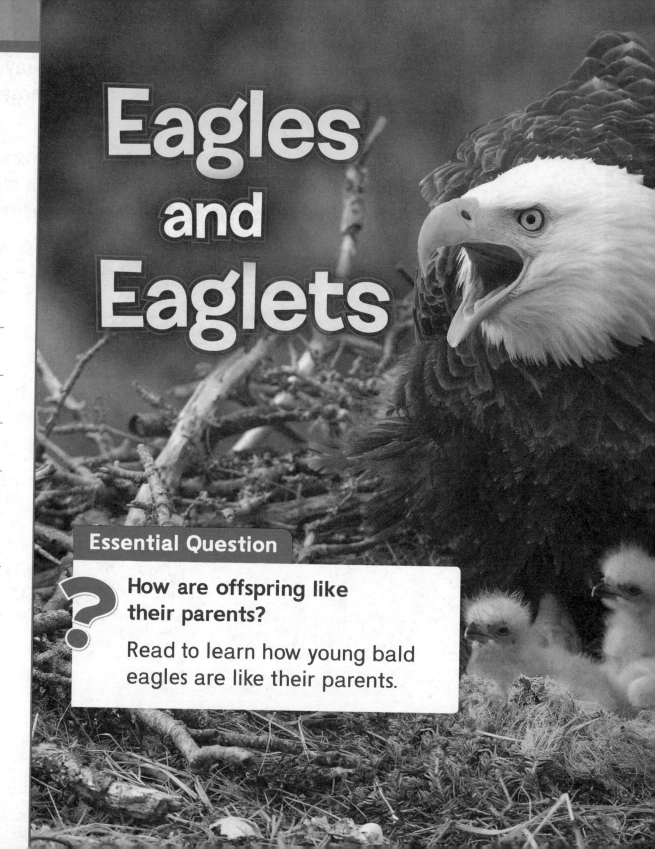

Eagles and Eaglets

Essential Question

How are offspring like their parents?

Read to learn how young bald eagles are like their parents.

Bald eagles are birds. The baby birds, or **offspring** are called eaglets. Let's read about how eaglets are like their parents.

It's Nesting Time

All birds lay eggs. Bald eagles build their nests in the tops of trees so the eggs will be safe. Their nests are built of sticks and grass. They add on to their nests each year. They can become huge! These **giant** nests can be as large as nine feet across. That's bigger than your bed!

The mother eagle lays from one to three eggs. She sits on her eggs until they hatch. Then both parents watch over the nest.

FIND TEXT EVIDENCE

Read

Paragraph 1
Reread
Reread and **underline** the sentence that explains what an eaglet is.

Paragraphs 2-3
Main Topic and Key Details
Circle the sentence that tells how eagles keep their eggs safe. What happens after the eggs hatch?

_____

_____

_____

Reread
Author's Craft

How does the author help you to picture the size of an eagle's nest?

FIND TEXT EVIDENCE

Read

Paragraph 1

Main Topic and Key Details

Underline two ways eaglets need their parents.

Paragraph 2

Reread

Circle what eagles use to hunt, fly, and catch fish.

Homographs

In the last sentence, does *live* mean "to happen now" or "to stay alive"?

_____

_____

Reread

Author's Craft

How does the author use description to show what an eaglet must learn?

Proud Parents

At first the eaglets are helpless. They cannot walk. They need their parents for food. They also cannot see well. Birds are not **mammals**. They do not have milk to feed their young. They hunt for food. Eaglets also need their parents for safety.

Eaglets Grow Up

Bald eagles use their sharp eyes to hunt. They use their strong wings to fly fast. They also use their claws and beak to catch fish. Young eaglets must learn all these things. Then they can live on their own.

The eagles must bring food to the eaglets.

Accent Alaska.com/Alamy Stock Photo

Unlike mammals, birds have feathers, not **fur**. An eaglet is born **covered** with soft gray down. It cannot fly until it grows dark feathers like its parents. The eaglet stays near the nest until its wings grow strong. That takes about five months.

Bald Eagle

powerful eyes

dark feathers on body and wings

hooked yellow beak

white tail feathers

long claws

Frank Leung/Getty Images

FIND TEXT EVIDENCE

Read

Main Topic and Key Details
Underline the text that tells when eaglets can fly. How long does it take for their wings to grow strong?

_____

_____

_____

Diagram and Labels
Circle the part of the diagram that shows what eagles use to fly.

Read

Reread

Underline the sentence that tells you when an eaglet becomes an adult. **Circle** how long this takes.

Fluency

Intonation Reread the page to a partner. Show that some words and phrases are important by reading them slowly. This will help you to express the meaning of the text to your partner.

Reread

Author's Craft

How does the author point out an important detail in the illustration?

An eaglet becomes an **adult** when it has learned to do all the things its parents do. This takes about five years. Bald eagles can stay **alive** for up to thirty years.

When the bald eagle soars, the feathers on its huge wings spread out like fingers.

Bald Eagles Soar

Once it learns to fly, the bald eagle can soar for hours. The bald eagle must take good care of its feathers. It uses its beak to **groom** itself. It must keep its feathers clean. Can you believe this powerful eagle began life as a helpless baby?

Ken Canning/Getty Images

FIND TEXT EVIDENCE

`Read`

Main Topic and Key Details
What can a bald eagle do once it learns to fly?

Homographs
Underline two sentences that help you understand the meaning of *groom*. What does an eagle use to groom its feathers?

`Reread`

Summarize

Use your notes and think about the key details in "Eagles and Eaglets." Then summarize how eaglets become adults.

Author's Craft

Reread the last sentence. How does the author use a question and word choice to make you think about key details in the text?

Vocabulary

**Talk with a partner about each word.
Then answer the questions.**

adult

My father is an **adult**.

Who are some adults that you know?

_____

_____

alive

I water the flowers to keep them **alive**.

What are some things that are alive?

_____

_____

covered

An eagle is **covered** with feathers.

What other birds are covered with feathers?

_____

_____

fur

My kitten has **fur** that is soft and fluffy.

Name some other animals that have fur.

_____

_____

giant

An elephant is a **giant** animal.

What other animals are giant?

_____

_____

Build Your Word List Reread the second paragraph on page 3. Circle *huge*. Write synonyms for *huge*. Use a thesaurus to help you.

groom

I use a brush to **groom** my dog.

How does a cat groom itself?

_____

_____

mammal

A **mammal** is an animal that has fur or hair and breathes air.

What mammals can you name?

_____

_____

offspring

The mother rabbit has two **offspring**.

What is the name for the offspring of a dog?

_____

Homographs

Homographs are words that are spelled the same but have different meanings and sometimes different pronunciations.

FIND TEXT EVIDENCE

I know down can mean "to go from high to low" or "fluffy feathers." Since eaglets are covered with down, the second meaning makes sense in this sentence.

An eaglet is born covered with soft gray (down.)

Your Turn Use clues on page 3 to figure out the meaning of _hatch_ in this sentence:

"She sits on her eggs until they hatch."

_____

_____

Takayuki Maekawa/The Image Bank/Getty Images

Reread

As you read, you may come across new words or information you don't understand. You can reread to help you understand the text.

 FIND TEXT EVIDENCE

On page 4 of "Eagles and Eaglets," the text tells how birds are helpless. I will go back and reread to understand why they are helpless.

Page 4

At first the eaglets are helpless. They cannot walk. They need their parents for food. They also cannot see well. Birds are not **mammals**. They do not have milk to feed their young. They hunt for food. Eaglets also need their parents for safety.

I reread that eaglets cannot walk, so they need their parents to get them food. This explains why they are helpless.

 Your Turn Why are eagles not able to fly when they are born? Reread page 5 to find the answer.

_____

_____

Diagram and Labels

The selection "Eagles and Eaglets" is an expository text. It gives facts about a topic and has text features.

FIND TEXT EVIDENCE

I know that "Eagles and Eaglets" is an expository text because it gives facts about eagles. It also has text features that help me learn about eagles. I see a diagram and labels.

Page 5

Unlike mammals, birds have feathers, not **fur**. An eaglet is born **covered** with soft gray down. It cannot fly until it grows dark feathers like its parents. The eaglet stays near the nest until its wings grow strong. That takes about five months.

Bald Eagle

dark feathers on body and wings

white tail feathers

powerful eyes

hooked yellow beak

long claws

Frank Leung/Getty Images

Diagram
A diagram is a picture that shows information.

Labels
The labels explain parts of the diagram.

COLLABORATE

Your Turn What did you learn about eagles from looking at the diagram and reading the labels?

_____

_____

_____

Frank Leung/Getty Images

Main Topic and Key Details

The main topic is what the selection is about. Key details give information about the main topic.

🔍 **FIND TEXT EVIDENCE**

As I read page 3, I learn that I will be reading about eagles and eaglets. This must be the main topic. I also read about eagle's nests and eggs.

Main Topic
Eagles and Eaglets
Key Detail
Eagles build nests and lay eggs.

 Your Turn Continue reading the text. Fill in the graphic organizer with more key details that tell about the topic.

Steve Shuey/Alamy

> **Quick Tip**
>
> Think about what the author wants you to learn or understand about the topic. This will help you identify a key detail in a paragraph or section of text.

Main Topic Eagles and Eaglets		
Key Detail	**Key Detail**	**Key Detail**
Eagles build nests and lay eggs.		

Respond to Reading

Talk about the prompt below. Think about how the author presents key details in the selection. Use your notes and graphic organizer.

How does the author use facts and text features to explain how an eaglet becomes an eagle?

_____

_____

_____

_____

_____

_____

_____

_____

Identify and Gather Sources

Relevant sources can be books, magazine articles, or websites. To find a reliable source, make sure the author's purpose is to teach readers about a topic.

What would be a relevant source to study alligators?

Find a relevant source on the Internet to study zebras. Write it below.

_____

Examples of reliable sources on the Internet are school websites that end in ".edu" or government websites that end in ".gov." Avoid doing research on websites that try to convince you of an opinion.

_____

_____

Life Cycle Diagram With a partner, create a diagram about the life cycle of an insect. Use reliable sources to research the stages of the insect's life. Draw the life cycle and describe each stage.

My insect is _____

Reliable sources for my research _____

_____

Baby Bears

? **How does the author use photographs and captions to help you understand bear families?**

Literature Anthology:
pages 110–127

Talk About It Talk about the details in the photographs and captions on pages 118–119.

Make Inferences

Think about what bears must learn to live on their own. What inference can you make about why bear cubs need to learn to climb trees?

Cite Text Evidence Write what you learn about bear families from the text, photographs, and caption.

Text	Photographs	Caption

Write The author uses photographs and captions _____

_____

_____

How does the author use headings to show how the text is organized?

Talk About It Reread page 120. Talk about the question the heading at the top of the page asks.

Cite Text Evidence Write the heading on page 120. Then write details from this part, or section, of the text.

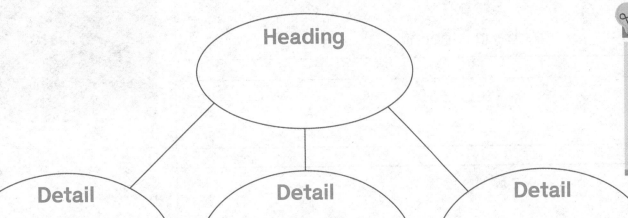

Write The author uses headings to show _____

_____

_____

? **How does the diagram help you understand how baby bears become adult bears?**

Talk About It Reread page 124. Talk about how a cub becomes an adult.

Cite Text Evidence Write the steps in a bear's life cycle.

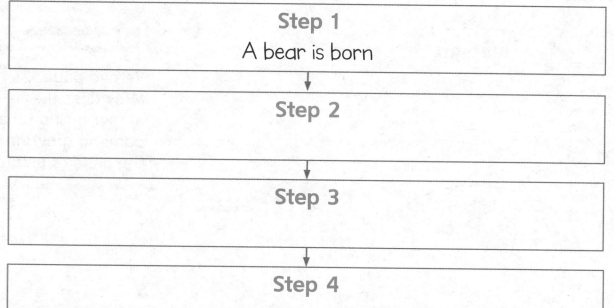

Step 1
A bear is born

↓

Step 2

↓

Step 3

↓

Step 4

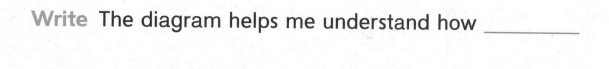

Write The diagram helps me understand how _____

_____

_____

Respond to Reading

Discuss the prompt below. Think about the purpose of text features like headings and diagrams.

How does the author organize the information to help you understand how bears grow?

_____

_____

_____

_____

_____

_____

_____

Quick Tip

Use these sentence frames to organize your text evidence.

The author organizes the information by...

The author explains in "Bear families"...

The diagram shows...

Self-Selected Reading

Choose a text. Read the first two pages. If you don't understand five or more words, choose another text. Fill in your writer's notebook with the title, author, genre, and your purpose for reading.

From Caterpillar to Butterfly

A butterfly is not a mammal. It does not have live babies or feed milk to its young. A butterfly is an insect. It lays eggs.

Lee Canfield/SuperStock

Literature Anthology: pages 128-129

Reread the title and text. What does the title tell you about the main topic of the selection?

_____

_____

_____

_____

_____

Circle details that explain what a butterfly is.

COLLABORATE

Discuss the photo on the page. What does it show? How does the photo support the main topic?

Butterfly Life Cycle

1. Egg
The adult butterfly lays an egg on a milkweed leaf.

2. Larva
After 3 or 4 days, a tiny caterpillar comes out of the egg. Caterpillars are a kind of larva. The caterpillar eats its shell for food.

5. Adult
Two weeks later, an adult butterfly comes out of the chrysalis. It will lay an egg on a leaf, and the cycle will continue.

4. Chrysalis
The caterpillar forms a shell around itself. The shell is called a chrysalis.

3. Caterpillar
For about two weeks, the caterpillar eats leaves and grows bigger.

Reread the page. What happens first in the life cycle of a butterfly? How do you know?

_____

_____

_____

_____

_____

Reread step 4. **Underline** the sentence that tells what a chrysalis is. **Circle** the chrysalis in the picture.

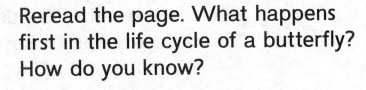

COLLABORATE

Discuss how the writer organizes the information in a diagram. Use text evidence to support your response.

(cw from top) Ed Reschke/Photolibrary/Photolibrary/Getty Images; Don Johnston_IH/Alamy; U.S. Fish & Wildlife Service; Don Johnston_IH/Alamy; Ingram Publishing/Alamy

? **What is the author's purpose for writing "From Caterpillar to Butterfly"?**

Talk About It Reread page 21. Why are the parts of the diagram numbered? What do the parts show?

Cite Text Evidence Write clues in the diagram of a butterfly life cycle that show the author's purpose.

Clue	Clue

Author's Purpose

Write The author's purpose in writing "From Caterpillar to Butterfly" is _____

_____

_____

Lisa Thornberg/E+/Getty Images

Diagrams

Authors can use diagrams to show how parts of something work together. Life cycle diagrams show and tell how living things grow and change.

FIND TEXT EVIDENCE

Look back at the butterfly life cycle diagram again on page 21. Take notes on each step on the lines below.

1. _____

2. _____

3. _____

4. _____

5. Two weeks later, an adult butterfly comes out.

Your Turn Why does the author show the life cycle of a butterfly in a circle?

_____

_____

You can use diagrams to explain key details and show how they are connected. Adding arrows and numbers to your diagram can help show how the parts work together or follow a sequence.

? **What does the photograph of the sculpture help you understand? How are these ideas similar to what you learned in "Eagles and Eaglets" and *Baby Bears*?**

Talk About It Talk about the sculpture and caption. What does the artist show about a mother lion and her cubs, or offspring?

Cite Text Evidence In the caption, **underline** a clue that tells how long the cubs need their mother.

Write The selections I read and the sculpture and caption help me understand how baby animals

_____

_____

_____

_____

_____

> **Quick Tip**
>
> Use these sentence starters as you talk about the sculpture and answer the question:
>
> *Baby animals need their parents for...*
>
> *The offspring, or babies, must learn...*

The artist shows lion cubs clinging to their mother. The cubs need her until they learn to hunt for themselves.

Present Your Work

COLLABORATE

With your partner, plan how you will present your Life Cycle Diagram to the class. Use the Presenting Checklist to help you improve your presentation. Discuss the sentence starters below and write your answers.

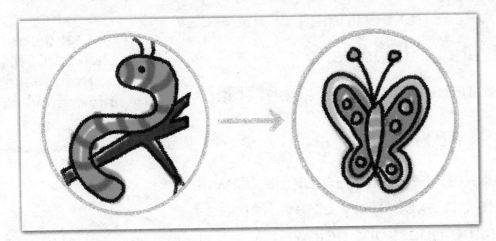

An interesting fact I learned about the life cycle is

_____

_____

I would like to know more about how the insect

_____

_____

Quick Tip

Decide the parts of the diagram you and your partner will each present. Practice moving smoothly from one part to the next.

✓ Presenting Checklist

☐ Practice in front of a friend.

☐ Present the stages in the life cycle of the insect in order.

☐ Speak clearly and slowly so the class can understand the diagram.

☐ Make eye contact with your audience.

☐ Cite the reliable sources you used.

Literature Anthology: pages 110–127

Expert Model

Features of Expository Essay

An expository essay is a type of expository text. It gives ideas and information about a topic.

- It introduces the topic in the beginning of the essay.

- It has facts that tell about the topic.

- It can have a text structure that tells about things in order.

Word Wise

The author uses one sentence for each fact. This helps to make the information clear to the reader.

Analyze an Expert Model Studying *Baby Bears* will help you learn to write an expository essay. Reread pages 112–113. Answer the questions below.

How does the author grab your attention?

_____

How does the author introduce the main topic of baby bears?

_____

_____

Plan: Brainstorm

Generate Ideas You will write an expository essay that tells how a baby animal grows. Use this space for your ideas. Brainstorm words that describe baby animals and draw pictures.

Life on White/Photodisc/Getty Images

Plan: Choose Your Topic

Writing Prompt Write an expository essay that explains how a baby animal grows. Go back to the ideas about baby animals that you brainstormed on page 27. Choose one of these animals to write about. Complete these sentences to help you get started.

My baby animal is _____

_____

I already know that _____

_____

I will look for other facts about this animal in _____

_____

Purpose and Audience Authors write expository essays to teach readers about the world. Think about why you chose the baby animal to write about. Then explain your purpose for writing in your writer's notebook.

> **Quick Tip**
>
> Your audience, or readers, may include your classmates. Think about how to interest your readers and what you want them to learn from your essay.

> **Word Wise**
>
> Thinking about your audience will help you decide the words and tone to use in your writing. Use formal language when you are writing for a serious purpose, such as for expository essays, reports, and letters to your teacher.

tiirc83/E+/Getty Images

Plan: Research

COLLABORATE

Generate Questions Authors often plan their writing by asking questions about a topic. Look at the chart below. An author researched facts about a baby puffin bird. The author asked questions about the baby bird first and used the answers in an expository essay.

Read the answers in the chart. Use these facts to complete the questions.

Question	Answer
What are the babies _____ ?	The babies are called pufflings.
_____ does the baby eat?	The parents feed them fish.
_____ does the baby change as it grows?	The baby's dark beak turns orange.

Plan In your writer's notebook, make a Question and Answer chart like the one above. Think about what sources you can use to find the answers. Use reliable sources, such as books, magazines, and websites.

Draft

Order Ideas The author of "Eagles and Eaglets" describes events in an eaglet's life. Reread pages 5–6. These events can be put into a Sequence Chart. Complete this Sequence Chart.

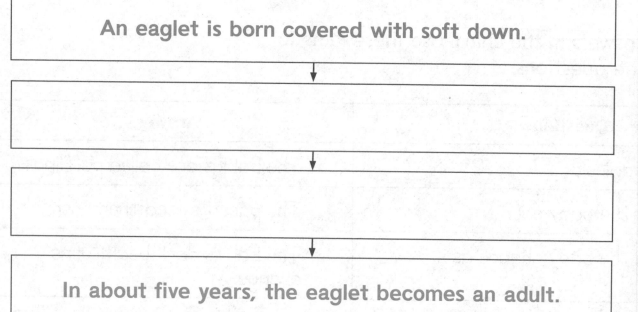

An eaglet is born covered with soft down.

↓

↓

↓

In about five years, the eaglet becomes an adult.

Write a Draft Make a Sequence Chart in your writer's notebook. Use reliable sources such as books, magazines, and websites. Look over your list of questions. Then use this information to write your draft.

Revise

Sentence Fluency Writers use short and long sentences to add interest. Read the paragraph below. Use descriptive words and details to revise it. Make sure you use both short and long sentences to make the writing more interesting.

> Eagles build nests. Eagles lay eggs. The mother sits on her eggs.
>
> The eggs hatch. The parents watch the nest.

_____

_____

_____

_____

_____

 Revise It's time to revise your draft. Make sure you have some short sentences and some longer sentences to keep your writing interesting.

Revise: Peer Conferences

Review a Draft Listen carefully as a partner reads his or her work aloud. Begin by telling what you like about the draft. Make suggestions that you think will make the writing stronger.

Partner Feedback Write one of your partner's suggestions that you will use in the revision of your text.

Based on my partner's feedback, I will _____

_____

_____

After you finish giving each other feedback, reflect on the peer conference. What was helpful? What might you do differently next time?

_____

_____

Revision Use the Revising Checklist to help you figure out what text you may need to move, add to, or delete. Remember to use the rubric on page 35 to help you with your revision.

Remember to use the rubric on page 35 to help you with your revision.

Quick Tip

Use these sentence starters to discuss your partner's work.

The details in your draft helped me...

How about adding more facts about...

I have a question about...

 Revising Checklist

☐ Does my essay give facts in the correct order?

☐ Does it include words that show the correct order?

☐ Does it answer my questions about how a baby animal grows?

☐ Did I use both short and long sentences?

Edit and Proofread

When you **edit** and **proofread**, you look for and correct mistakes in your writing. Rereading a revised draft several times will help you catch any errors. Use the checklist below to edit your sentences.

Editing Checklist

- ☐ Do all sentences begin with a capital letter and end with a punctuation mark?
- ☐ Are nouns used correctly?
- ☐ Are plural nouns spelled correctly?
- ☐ Are commas used correctly?
- ☐ Are all the words spelled correctly?

List two mistakes you found as you proofread your text.

1 _____

_____

2 _____

_____

Tech Tip

When you type your text, choose a font that is easy to read. Usually, type that looks like print in a book is easier to read.

Grammar Connections

As you proofread, make sure the nouns you used are spelled correctly. Remember how the spellings of irregular plural nouns change, such as *child/children, man/men,* or *foot/feet.*

Publish, Present, and Evaluate

Publishing Create a neat, clean final copy of your Expository Essay. As you write your draft, be sure to print neatly and legibly. You may add illustrations, a diagram, or other visuals to make your published work more interesting.

Presentation Practice your presentation when you are ready to present your work. Use the Presenting Checklist to help you.

Evaluate After you publish and present your expository text, use the rubric on the next page to evaluate your writing.

✓ Presenting Checklist

- ☐ Sit up or stand up straight.
- ☐ Look at the audience.
- ☐ Speak slowly and clearly.
- ☐ Speak loudly so that everyone can hear you.
- ☐ Answer questions using facts from your essay.

1 What did you do successfully? _____

_____

_____

2 What needs more work? _____

_____

_____

Listening When you listen actively, you pay close attention to what you hear. When you listen to other students' presentations, take notes to help you better understand their ideas.

What I learned from ....'s presentation:

_____

Questions I have about ....'s presentation:

_____

4	3	2	1
• uses factual information to tell how a baby animal grows • follows a clear sequence and uses signal words • has a variety of sentence lengths • is free or almost free of errors	• uses mostly factual information to tell how a baby animal grows • follows a sequence and uses some signal words • has some variety in sentence length • has few errors	• uses some factual information • does not have a clear sequence and is missing signal words • has limited variety in sentence length • has many errors that distract from the meaning of the essay	• does not have much factual information • has a confusing order • has no variety in sentence length • has many errors that make the essay hard to understand

Essential Question

What can animals in stories teach us?

Do you know the story of the Tortoise and the Hare? Hare is ahead in a race with slow Tortoise. So, Hare takes a nap. As he sleeps, Tortoise moves ahead and wins the race!

Talk with a partner about how animals in stories can teach lessons. Speak clearly at a pace that makes sense. Write the lessons you might learn from this story in the word web.

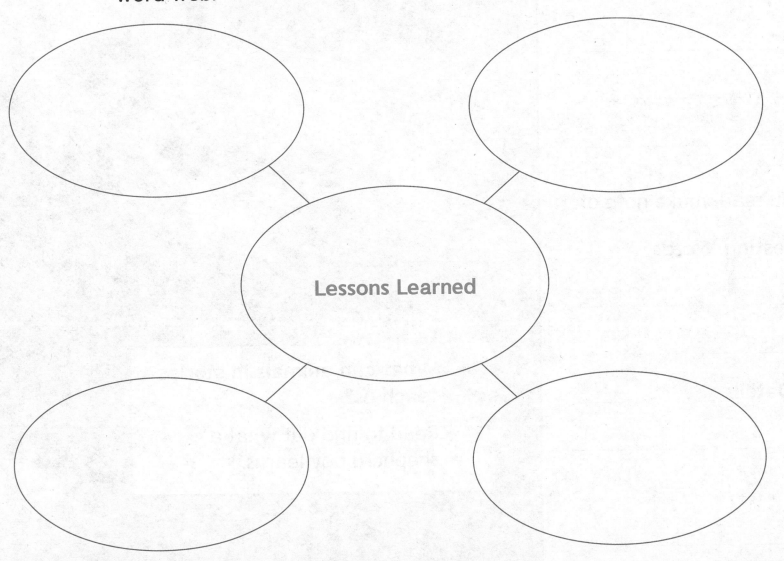

Lessons Learned

TAKE NOTES

Asking questions before you begin reading will help you understand the story. Write your questions here:

_____

_____

_____

As you read, make note of:

Interesting Words _____

_____

_____

Key Details _____

_____

_____

_____

The Boy Who Cried Wolf

Essential Question

?

What can animals in stories teach us?

Read to find out what a shepherd boy learns.

Long ago a shepherd boy sat on a hilltop watching the village sheep. He was not **fond** of his job. He didn't like it one bit. He would have liked something wonderful to happen, but nothing **remarkable** ever did.

The shepherd boy watched the clouds move softly by to stay busy. He saw horses, dogs, and dragons in the sky. He made up **stories** with these things as characters.

Peter Francis

FIND TEXT EVIDENCE

Read

Paragraph 1

Beginning, Middle, End

Underline the part that tells what job the shepherd boy is doing at the beginning of the story. What does he want?

_____

_____

Paragraph 1

Problem and Solution

Circle the sentence that tells what problem the shepherd boy has.

Reread

Author's Craft

What does the shepherd boy do to stay busy? Why does the author include this information?

FIND TEXT EVIDENCE 🔍

Read

Paragraph 2

Antonyms

Find and write the antonyms for the words below. **Circle** the two sets of antonyms in the story.

up _____

cry _____

Paragraph 2

Make, Confirm, Revise Predictions

What do you think the boy will do next?

_____

_____

Reread

Author's Craft

How do the text and illustrations show the villagers' feelings?

Then one day he had a better idea! He took a deep breath and cried out, "Wolf! Wolf! The wolf is chasing the sheep!"

The villagers ran up the hill to help the boy. When they got there, they saw no harmful wolf. The boy laughed. "Shepherd boy! Don't cry 'wolf!' unless there really is a wolf!" said the villagers. They went back down the hill.

That afternoon the boy again cried out, "Wolf! Wolf! The wolf is chasing the sheep!"

The villagers ran to help the boy again. They saw no wolf. The villagers were angry. "Don't cry 'wolf!' when there is NO WOLF!" they said. The shepherd boy just smiled. The villagers went quickly down the hill again.

FIND TEXT EVIDENCE 🔍

Read

Paragraphs 1-2

Problem and Solution

Underline the detail that shows the boy creating a problem. How do you know it's a problem?

_____

_____

_____

Paragraphs 1-2

Make, Confirm, Revise Predictions

What do you think will happen next?

_____

_____

_____

Peter Francis

FIND TEXT EVIDENCE

Read

Paragraph 1

Make, Confirm, Revise Predictions

Was your prediction from page 41 correct? Why or why not?

Paragraph 2

Beginning, Middle, End

Underline the sentence that explains what the sheep do at the end of the story. Why do they do this?

Reread

Author's Craft

How does the author use exclamation points to show how the boy feels?

That afternoon the boy saw a REAL wolf. He did not want the wolf to grab any of the sheep! The boy thought the wolf would **snatch** one of them for a **delicious**, tasty meal. A sheep would be a big **feast** for a wolf. He quickly jumped to his feet and cried, "WOLF! WOLF!" The villagers thought he was tricking them again, so they did not come.

That night the shepherd boy did not return with their sheep. The villagers found the boy weeping real tears. "There really was a wolf here!" he said. "The flock ran away! When I cried out, 'Wolf! Wolf!' no one came. Why didn't you come?"

A kind man talked to the boy as they walked slowly back to the village. "In the morning, we'll help you look for the sheep," he said. "You have just learned one of life's important **lessons**. This is something you need to know. Nobody **believes** a person who tells lies. It is always better to tell the truth!"

Summarize

Use the most important details from "The Boy Who Cried Wolf" to orally summarize what happens in the story.

FIND TEXT EVIDENCE 🔍

Read

Problem and Solution

Circle who helps the boy at the end of the story. How does he help?

_____

_____

Combine Information

Use details you already know to explain how the boy learns his lesson.

_____

_____

Reread

Author's Craft

What message does the author want to share in this fable?

Vocabulary

Talk with a partner about each word. Then answer the questions.

believe

We **believe** it is going to rain today.

What is something you believe will happen today?

_____

_____

delicious

We ate the **delicious** pizza.

Describe something that tastes delicious.

_____

_____

> **Build Your Word List** Reread the last paragraph on page 40. Circle _help_. Use a word web to write more forms of the word. Use a dictionary to help you.

feast

Our family has a **feast** on holidays.

When do you have a feast?

_____

_____

fond

Rob is very **fond** of his puppy.

What is something that you are fond of?

_____

_____

lessons

You learn important **lessons** from your family.

What lessons do you learn at school?

_____

_____

remarkable

I saw a **remarkable** rainbow after the rain.

Describe something that is remarkable.

_____

_____

snatch

My dog can **snatch** a ball out of the air.

Show how you would snatch something from your desk.

_____

_____

stories

Dad reads **stories** before bedtime.

What are some stories you like?

_____

_____

Antonyms

Antonyms are words that are opposite in meaning.

FIND TEXT EVIDENCE

As I read the end of the story, I see the words lies *and* truth. *These words have a completely different meaning. They help me understand the story.*

Nobody believes a person who tells lies. It is always better to tell the truth!

Your Turn Find the antonym for this word.

morning, page 43 _____

_____

Write your own sentence using a pair of antonyms.

Make, Confirm, Revise Predictions

Use what you read in the story to help you predict, or guess, what might happen next. As you read, check to see if your predictions are correct. If they are not correct, revise, or change, your predictions.

🔍 **FIND TEXT EVIDENCE**

On page 40 of "The Boy Who Cried Wolf," I made a prediction about the boy's actions and what he will do next.

Page 41

That afternoon the boy again cried out, "Wolf! Wolf! The wolf is chasing the sheep!"

The villagers ran to help the boy again. They saw no wolf. The villagers were angry.

On page 41, I confirmed my prediction by reading about how the villagers react.

Your Turn When the boy saw the wolf, what did you predict would happen? Reread the text on page 42 and find the text that confirmed your prediction.

Beginning, Middle, End

"The Boy Who Cried Wolf" is a fable. A fable is a made-up story that teaches a lesson. It has a beginning, middle, and end. It often has animals that act like humans.

FIND TEXT EVIDENCE

I can use what I read to tell that "The Boy Who Cried Wolf" is a fable. It is a made-up story that has a beginning, middle, and end.

Page 39

Long ago a shepherd boy sat on a hilltop watching the village sheep. He was not **fond** of his job. He didn't like it one bit. He would have liked something wonderful to happen, but nothing **remarkable** ever did.

The shepherd boy watched the clouds move softly by to stay busy. He saw horses, dogs, and dragons in the sky. He made up **stories** with these things as characters.

Readers to Writers

When you read a fable, ask yourself: *What happens in the beginning? In the middle? In the end?* A graphic organizer can help you organize and understand the story's events.

Beginning, Middle, End

In the beginning of the fable, we meet a shepherd boy and learn how he feels about his job.

COLLABORATE

Your Turn Tell what happens in the middle and at the end of the fable. What is important about the ending that makes it a fable?

_____

_____

_____

Problem and Solution

A story is often about the problem the characters are having. The solution is how the characters solve the problem by the end of the story.

 FIND TEXT EVIDENCE

As I read page 39 of "The Boy Who Cried Wolf," I see details in the illustrations and text that tell me about the problem the character is having. These details help me understand the story.

> **Quick Tip**
>
> As you read, look at the illustrations to help you understand the story. Remember the illustrations as you learn more about the problem and solution.

> **Problem**
>
> The shepherd boy is bored.

↓

Your Turn Continue rereading "The Boy Who Cried Wolf." Fill in the graphic organizer with the steps that lead to the solution, and then the solution.

Peter Francis

Problem

The shepherd boy is bored.

Steps to Solution

Solution

Respond to Reading

COLLABORATE

Talk about the prompt below. Think about how the author repeats some events in the story. Use your notes and graphic organizer.

How does the author show that the shepherd boy's feelings have changed at the end of the story?

_____

_____

_____

_____

_____

_____

_____

Quick Tip

Use these sentence starters to help you organize your text evidence.

At the beginning of the story, the boy feels...

In the middle of the story, the boy feels...

At the end of the story, the boy learns...

Grammar Connections

Remember that *villagers* is plural, so use the pronoun *they* to talk about the villagers.

SCIENCE

Cite Sources

When you do research, you gather information about a topic. To **cite sources** means to tell where you get this information from. If your information is from a book, tell who wrote the book, the title of the book, and the year the book is from.

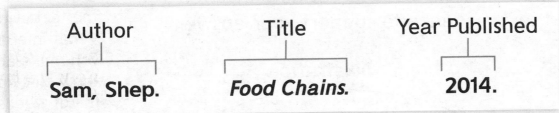

Author	Title	Year Published
Sam, Shep.	*Food Chains.*	**2014.**

What is the title in the source above?

_____

COLLABORATE

Wolf Food Chain Diagram With a partner, research wolves and what they eat. Then draw a diagram. Show and label all the animals in the wolf food chain.

What source will you use to help you draw your diagram? Write the author, title, and year of the source.

_____

_____

These wolves are looking for prey, such as a deer or moose, to eat.

Shutterstock/Michelle Lalancette

Wolf! Wolf!

Literature Anthology:
pages 130–153

? **How does the author help you understand how the wolf feels about the weeds in his garden?**

Talk About It Reread page 131. What do the words and the illustration tell you about how the wolf feels?

Cite Text Evidence Write clues about how the wolf is feeling. Find text evidence to support your answer.

Make Inferences

An inference is a best guess based on the text evidence. What inference can you make about why the wolf's garden is full of weeds?

Quick Tip

Identify the words that are similar in the *Words* and the *Illustration* circles. Include those words in the *Both* section.

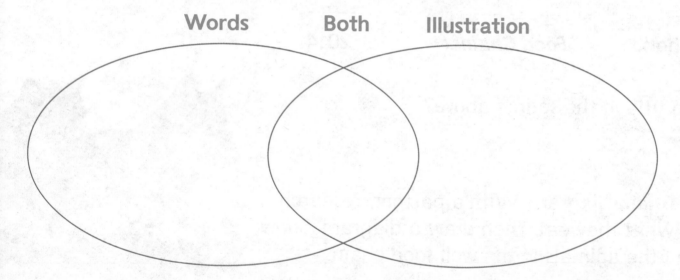

Words   Both   Illustration

Write The author helps me understand that the wolf _____

_____

_____

? **How does the author make it clear the wolf is planning to trick the boy?**

COLLABORATE

Talk About It Reread pages 144–145. Talk about what the wolf looks like and what he says when he meets the boy.

Cite Text Evidence Complete the chart. Write the clues that show you what the wolf is planning.

Illustration Clues	Text Clues

Write The author makes it clear that the wolf _____

_____

_____

Quick Tip

As you read, use these sentence starters to talk about how the wolf feels.

The wolf says...

The wolf wants...

 Combine Information

Use what you know about the wolf and how he feels to help you understand what the wolf is planning and why.

? **Why does the author repeat the phrase, "I'm a picky eater"?**

Talk About It Reread pages 145 and 149. Talk about what it means to be a picky eater.

Cite Text Evidence Write why both the wolf and the goat are picky eaters.

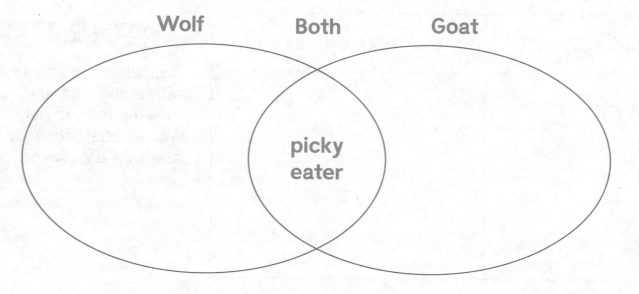

Wolf   Both   Goat

picky eater

Write The author repeats the phrase, "I'm a picky eater"

because _____

_____

_____

Respond to Reading

COLLABORATE

Discuss the prompt below. Think about what the wolf says, does, and feels in each part of the story.

How does the wolf change from the beginning of the story to the end?

_____

_____

_____

_____

_____

_____

_____

_____

_____

Quick Tip

Use these sentence starters to organize your text evidence.

At the beginning of the story, the wolf...

At the end of the story, the wolf...

Self-Selected Reading

Choose a text. In your writer's notebook, write the title, author, and genre of the book. As you read, make a connection to ideas in other texts you read, or a personal experience. Write your ideas in your writer's notebook.

Cinderella and Friends

Yeh-Shen's only friend is a beautiful fish. Every day, the fish comes out of the water to meet her. Yeh-Shen feeds the fish. When the fish dies, Yeh-Shen learns the fish bones are magical. Yeh-Shen makes a wish. She wants to go to the spring festival. The bones give her a beautiful dress and golden slippers to wear. At the festival, Yeh-Shen loses one of the slippers. The king finds the lost slipper. He says that he wants to marry the owner of the slipper. Many people try on the golden slipper. It only fits Yeh-Shen. She and the king become married, and they live happily ever after.

Alex Steele-Morgan

Literature Anthology: pages 154–157

Reread the story. **Circle** the clue that explains why Yeh-Shen might be sitting by the river. How does the author use the illustration to help tell the story?

_____

_____

Draw a box around how Yeh-Shen is a good friend to the fish.

How does the fish help Yeh-Shen? **Underline** the clue.

COLLABORATE

Talk with a partner about why it is important to help a friend who has a problem.

Rhodopis is a poor servant girl. Her only friends are the birds, hippos, and monkeys along the river. Rhodopis likes to sing and dance for them. The birds eat from her hand. A monkey sometimes sits on her shoulder. They love her. One evening, a bird snatches her slipper away. The bird flies over the king's castle and drops the slipper onto his throne. The king searches to find the owner of the slipper. When he finds Rhodopis, they fall in love and she becomes the queen.

Reread the story. **Underline** a clue about how Rhodopis is a good friend to the animals. What does this tell you about Rhodopis?

She is Kind.

Circle what happens to Rhodopis at the end of the story. Explain how her animal friends helped her and the king meet.

The bird drops her slipper on

COLLABORATE

Talk with a partner about how Yeh-Shen and Rhodopis are similar. How are they different?

Alex Steele-Morgan

? **Why does the author tell you about these two stories from "Cinderella and Friends"?**

COLLABORATE

Talk About It Reread pages 56–57. Talk about what the two stories have in common.

Cite Text Evidence Write details from each story that help you understand how animals can be good friends.

Yeh-Shen	Rhodopis

Write The author tells these two stories to show

_____

_____

_____

Evaluate Information

Read each story carefully to identify what happens in the beginning, middle, and end. What happens to the main characters?

Compare and Contrast

Authors of expository texts often use a specific text structure to organize their information. For example, they might use a text structure that compares and contrasts two or more examples.

FIND TEXT EVIDENCE

Look at pages 154–157. Describe how the author organizes the information to make it easy to compare and contrast the different stories. _____

_____

_____

_____

 Your Turn Why did the author organize "Cinderella and Friends" to include stories from different parts of the world? Write your answer on the lines below.

_____

_____

_____

? What lessons can animals in the stories you read or stories that are acted out teach you?

COLLABORATE

Talk About It Talk about what animal faces you see in the photograph. Why is it helpful to see what animal characters look like when a story is acted out?

Cite Text Evidence In the caption, **underline** the purpose of the masks. **Circle** one of the masks. Tell your partner how the mask can be used to tell stories.

Write From the animal masks and the animal characters in the selections I read, I learn

_____

_____

_____

_____

_____

_____

_____

Storytellers in Panama use animal masks like these to help tell stories.

Present Your Work

COLLABORATE

With your partner, plan how you will present your food chain to the class. Discuss the sentence starters below and write your answers.

I learned that wolves eat _____

_____

_____

_____

The arrows in the diagram show _____

_____

_____

_____

✔ Presenting Checklist

- ☐ Decide how you and your partner will take turns presenting the information in the diagram.
- ☐ Listen as your partner speaks.
- ☐ Stay on topic. Talk only about your part of the presentation.
- ☐ Listen carefully to questions from your classmates.

Talk About It

Jeffrey L. Rotman/Corbis Documentary/Getty Images

This dolphin is large, wet, and makes whistling sounds. We can use words to describe how an animal looks, feels, sounds, and smells. We can explain how animals behave and express themselves.

Use sensory words to talk with a partner about an animal that you like. Write your ideas on the web.

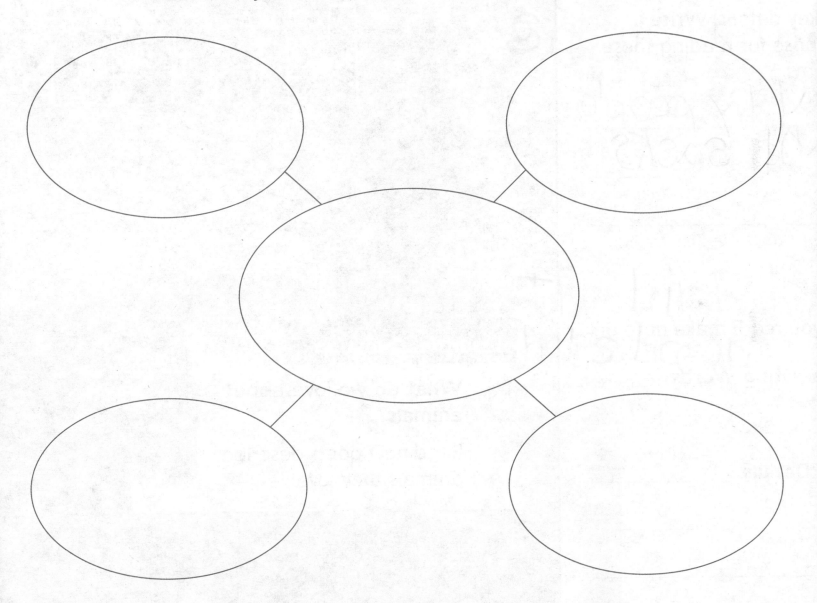

TAKE NOTES
Knowing why you are reading a text can help you recognize or focus on key details. Write a purpose for reading these poems.

_____

_____

_____

_____

As you read, make note of:

Interesting Words _____

_____

Key Details _____

_____

_____

Cats and Kittens

Essential Question

?

What do we love about animals?

Read how poets describe animals they love.

Martin Poole/Digital Vision/Getty Images; (mouse) D. Hurst/Alamy

Cats and kittens express their views
With hisses, purrs, and little mews.

Instead of taking baths like me,
They use their tongues quite handily.

I wonder what my mom would say
If I tried cleaning up that way.

They stay as still as still can be,
Until a mouse they chance to see.

And then in one great flash of fur
They pounce on a toy with a PURRRR.

– by Constance Keremes

FIND TEXT EVIDENCE

Read

Lines 3–6
Key Details
Underline the detail that tells how cats get clean. What does the narrator think about this?

If people tried

Lines 5–8
Rhyme

Circle the words that rhyme in lines 5–6. Then **draw a box** around words that rhyme in lines 7-8.

Reread
Author's Craft

How does the poet help the reader understand what kittens sound like?

FIND TEXT EVIDENCE

Read

Lines 1–2

Key Details

Write the detail that tells how the humps on camels can be used.

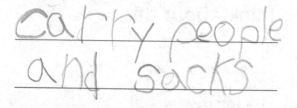

carry people and sacks

Lines 5–6

Suffixes

Circle the word ending in the word that means "jump up and down." **Underline** what the word shows about the camels.

Reread

Author's Craft

How does the poet show her feelings about camels?

Desert Camels

Camels have a hump on their backs
To carry people and their sacks.

They're very strong, don't mind the Sun,
Won't stop for drinks until they're done.

They give people a bouncy ride.
They sway and move from side to side.

I'd like a camel for a pet,
But haven't asked my mother yet!

— by Martine Wren

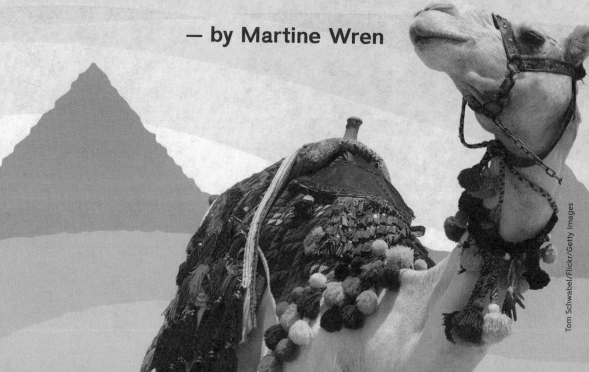

Tom Schwabel/Flickr/Getty Images

A Bat Is Not a Bird

A bat has neither feathers nor beak.
He does not chirp, just gives a shriek.

He flies by hearing sounds like pings,
Flapping, flapping his leathery wings.

At night when I'm asleep in my bed,
He gets to fly around instead!

— by Trevor Reynolds

Make Connections

Describe how you would behave with your favorite animal. How would the animal respond to you?

FIND TEXT EVIDENCE 🔍

Read

Lines 1–2
Key Details
Draw a box around the details that describe how a bat looks different from a bird.

Line 3
Rhythm
Underline each beat in Line 3. How many beats are in that line?

8 beats

Reread
Author's Craft

How does the poet make a connection between the title of the poem and lines 1–2?

Vocabulary

Talk with a partner about each word. Then answer the questions.

behave

The boy is teaching his dog to **behave**.

How do you behave when you are in the library?

_____

_____

flapping

The robin was **flapping** its wings quickly.

What bird have you seen flapping its wings?

_____

_____

Build Your Word List Pick a word from one of the poems and make a word web of different forms of the word.

express

The dog wags its tail to **express** how it feels.

How do you express your feelings?

_____

_____

feathers

A peacock is covered in colorful **feathers**.

Where else have you seen feathers?

_____

_____

Poetry Words

poem

A **poem** is a form of writing that expresses imagination or feelings.

Would you rather read a poem or a story? Why?

_____

_____

rhyme

When two words **rhyme**, they have the same ending sound.

What is a word that rhymes with cat?

_____

_____

rhythm

Rhythm is the repeating accents, or beats, in a poem.

Why would a poet want a poem to have rhythm?

_____

_____

word choice

Word choice is the use of rich, colorful, exact words.

What word choice describes your favorite food?

_____

_____

Suffixes

A suffix is a word part or syllable added to the end of a word. You can separate the root word from a suffix, such as light•ly, to figure out what the word means.

🔍 FIND TEXT EVIDENCE

I'm not sure what the word handily *means. The dictionary says that handy means "easy to use or handle." The suffix —ly means "like or characteristic of." I think the word* handily *means "like something easy to handle."*

They use their tongues quite handily.

Your Turn Use the suffix to figure out the meaning of this word from the poem "A Bat Is Not a Bird."

leathery, page 67 _____

_____

Martin Poole/Digital Vision/Getty Images

Rhythm

Poems have a rhythm. Rhythm is the repeating accents in a poem. You can clap the rhythm, or beats, in a poem.

FIND TEXT EVIDENCE

Reread "Desert Camels" and listen to the beats in each line. Think about why the poet uses rhythm.

Quick Tip

To find the beats in a line, clap and count the syllables as you say each word.

Page 66

Camels have a hump on their backs
To carry people and their sacks.

They're very strong, don't mind the Sun,
Won't stop for drinks until they're done.

I clap the beats in the first line. There are eight beats. There are also eight beats in the second line. The beats make the poem fun to read.

Your Turn Clap the beats in the first two lines of "Cats and Kittens" and "Desert Camels." Are the rhythms the same or different?

_____

_____

_____

Rhyme

A rhyming poem has words that end with the same sounds. It tells a poet's thoughts or feelings.

🔍 FIND TEXT EVIDENCE

I can tell that "Cats and Kittens" is a rhyming poem. The author tells her thoughts about cats. Also, there are pairs of words that rhyme in the poem.

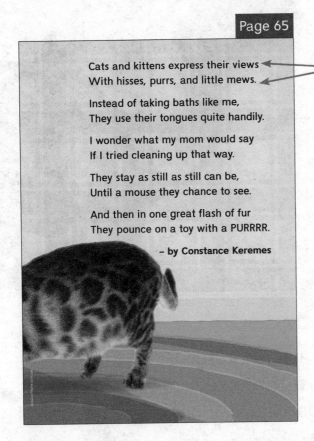

Page 65

Cats and kittens express their views
With hisses, purrs, and little mews.

Instead of taking baths like me,
They use their tongues quite handily.

I wonder what my mom would say
If I tried cleaning up that way.

They stay as still as still can be,
Until a mouse they chance to see.

And then in one great flash of fur
They pounce on a toy with a PURRRR.

– by Constance Keremes

Sometimes pairs of lines **rhyme** in a rhyming poem.

 Your Turn Which lines of "Desert Camels" rhyme? How do you know?

_____

_____

_____

_____

_____

Key Details

Key details give important information about a poem or story. You can find important information in the words, pictures, or photos.

🔍 **FIND TEXT EVIDENCE**

As I read "Desert Camels," I understand that camels are very strong. I read that they can carry people and their sacks.

> **Quick Tip**
>
> To decide if a detail is important, ask yourself if it helps you understand more about the main topic.

Detail
Camels can carry heavy loads.

 Your Turn Reread "Desert Camels." Pay attention to important details from the poem. Then list these key details from the poem in the graphic organizer.

Detail	Detail	Detail
Camels can carry heavy loads.		

Respond to Reading

Talk about the prompt below. Think about the key details and words that the poets use to describe each animal. Use your notes and graphic organizer. Try to include the vocabulary words in your response.

How does each poet show what is special about the animals in the poems?

_____

_____

_____

_____

_____

_____

_____

Quick Tip

Use these sentence starters to help you organize your text evidence.

The poet thinks cats are special because...

The poet thinks camels are special because...

The poet thinks bats are special because...

Grammar Connections

Commas are used to show a brief pause. Remember to use commas between two or more adjectives and to separate items in a series.

Generate Questions

Before you do your research, you need to think about questions you would like to answer. After you **generate questions**, look for facts and information about a topic.

Your questions will start with question words. What are the 6 question words?

W _____? W _____?

W _____? W _____?

W _____? H _____?

| What do most bats eat? |
| Where do bats sleep? |
| How do bats _____? |

These are some questions a student wrote before starting to research. Think about how the questions relate to the topic. What is the last question the student could ask?

_____

_____

Animal Information Cards Choose two animals you have read about this week. Come up with 3–5 questions to research about the animals. Then create information cards. On one side of the card, draw the animal. On the other side, describe the animal. Write two questions below to get started.

_____

_____

_____

Beetles, The Little Turtle

? **How do the poets arrange the lines to show different visual patterns in the poems?**

Literature Anthology: pages 158–160

Talk About It Reread pages 159–160. Look at how the lines are placed. What patterns do you see?

Cite Text Evidence Write what you learned about how the poems look alike and different. Use the Venn diagram below.

Quick Tip

A visual pattern happens more than once. You can see a pattern by looking at how the poet places a line or puts lines together in groups.

Beetles   Both   The Little Turtle

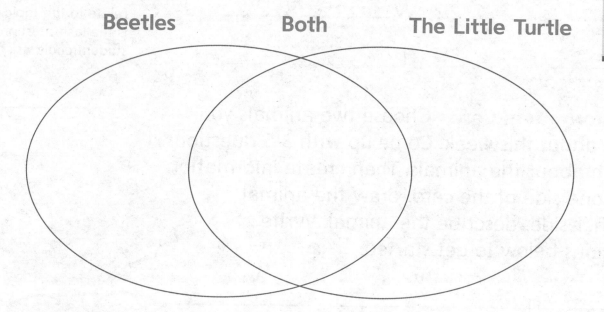

Write The lines are arranged to show _____

_____

? **How does the poet use words to create rhythm in "The Little Turtle"?**

Talk About It Read the poem "The Little Turtle" aloud with a partner. Talk about how the poem sounds.

Cite Text Evidence Write the words that repeat and the words that rhyme in each stanza.

Words that Repeat	Words that Rhyme
Stanza 1: _____	Stanza 1: _____
Stanza 2: _____	Stanza 2: _____
Stanza 3: _____	Stanza 3: _____

Write The poet creates rhythm by _____

_____

_____

_____

Respond to Reading

COLLABORATE Discuss the prompt below. Think about what the poets tell you about the creatures. Also think about how they present the information.

What about these creatures inspires the poets to write about them? How do they show it?

_____

_____

_____

_____

_____

_____

_____

_____

Gray Goose

Literature Anthology: pages 162–163

? **How does the poet use rhythm to help you understand how the gray goose moves and feels?**

COLLABORATE

Talk About It Talk about the fast rhythm of this poem. How does it fit with how the mama goose is feeling?

Cite Text Evidence Write the words and phrases that describe how the mama goose moves in this poem.

Quick Tip

The illustrations can help you figure out and learn words you don't know.

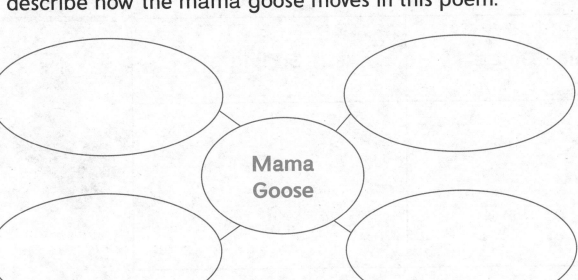

Mama Goose

Write The poet uses rhythm to help show

_____

_____

? **How does the poet compare and contrast the mother goose and her gosling?**

COLLABORATE

Talk About It Reread page 162 and talk about what the mama goose does. What does the gosling do?

Cite Text Evidence Write the words describing the mama goose and the words describing the gosling in the chart below.

Quick Tip

Read the poem aloud. Pay attention to how the words sound. The words about the mama goose can make you feel different than the words about the gosling.

Mama Goose	Gosling

Write The poet compares and contrasts the mother goose and her gosling by showing _____

_____

_____

Structures and Patterns

Quick Tip

As you read a poem, make a very short pause at the end of each line.

Poems are visually different from other kinds of writing. Poems are made up of lines instead of sentences and paragraphs. The patterns and structures are different.

FIND TEXT EVIDENCE

Take another look at the poem "The Gray Goose" on page 162. What do you notice about how the lines in this poem are arranged?

Readers to Writers

When you write your rhyming poem, the way you arrange the lines will affect how it looks and how it sounds.

_____

_____

_____

Your Turn Read "The Gray Goose" out loud to your partner. Then listen to your partner read the poem. Why do you think the poet arranged the lines of the poem this way?

COLLABORATE

_____

_____

_____

? How do the poets of the poems you read help you understand how they feel about the animals?

Talk About It Talk about what the speaker of "The Cow" loves about the animal.

Cite Text Evidence Circle the sensory words in "The Cow."

Write The poets of "Beetles," "Gray Goose," and "The Cow" use sensory

words to _____

_____

_____

_____

_____

_____

_____

The Cow

The friendly cow all red and white,
    I love with all my heart:
She gives me cream with all her might,
    To eat with apple-tart.

She wanders lowing here and there,
    And yet she cannot stray,
All in the pleasant open air,
    The pleasant light of day;

And blown by all the winds that pass
    And wet with all the showers,
She walks among the meadow grass
    And eats the meadow flowers.

—by Robert Louis Stevenson

Expression

When you read a poem aloud, use your voice to express your emotions. You can change your speed, volume, and tone of voice to show how a poem makes you feel. You can also use your voice to show important or surprising ideas.

Page 65

Cats and kittens express their views
With hisses, purrs, and little mews.

Instead of taking baths like me,
They use their tongues quite handily.

Use your voice to make "hisses" sound like a hiss. You can also say "little mews" more quietly than the other words.

Quick Tip

You can use your face and body to show how you feel when you read a poem aloud. You might smile when you read a funny part. Or try dropping your shoulders when you read a sad part.

Your Turn Turn back to page 67. Take turns reading "A Bat is Not a Bird" with a partner. Use your voice to express your feelings and to point out important ideas as you read. Afterward, think about how you did. Complete these sentences.

I remembered to _____

Next time I will _____

Expert Model

Features of a Rhyming Poem

Literature Anthology: page 160

A rhyming poem:

- has words that end with the same sounds.

- tells a poet's thoughts or feelings.

Analyze an Expert Model Studying "The Little Turtle" will help you learn how to write rhyming poems. Reread page 160 in the **Literature Anthology**. Answer the questions below.

In the first four lines of the poem, what two words rhyme?

_____

_____

What is the funny joke that the poet makes at the end of the poem?

_____

_____

Plan: Brainstorm

Generate Ideas You will write a rhyming poem about an animal. Use this space for your ideas. Draw animals that help you think of what your poem will be about. Then write words that tell about some of the animals.

Plan: Choose Your Topic

Writing Prompt Write a poem about an animal. Try to tell a story about the animal in your poem. Your poem should have at least four lines and rhyming words. Complete these sentences to help you get started.

The animal in my poem is _____

_____

My animal wants to _____

_____

A problem might be _____

_____

Purpose and Audience Authors write rhyming poems because they want to entertain their readers or share feelings. Think about what feeling you want your audience to have when they read your poem. Explain the feelings you want your readers to have in your writer's notebook.

> **Quick Tip**
>
> Your audience, or readers, may include your classmates or family. Most people like to read rhyming poems. As you write, think about why your audience will enjoy reading your poem.

Plan: Word Choice

Precise Language When you write, include details about your topic that will create a clear picture for your reader. Precise words are exact words that make your meaning clear. Complete the word bank below by writing precise words that describe a fish.

Word Bank		
splashing	scaly	smelly
slippery	glimmering	fast
golden	gliding	slimy

 Plan In your writer's notebook, use a word bank like the one found above. Fill it in with precise words about the animal in your poem.

Shutterstock/Vangert

Draft

Specific Details The author of "Gray Goose" gives many specific details to describe the goose and the baby. She includes details such as *webbed feet slapping* and *wild waddle*. These details make it easy to picture the goose. Notice the details the author includes about the gosling.

Now use this poem as a model to include specific details about the animal in your poem. Include words that rhyme as you describe the animal in your poem.

_____

_____

_____

_____

_____

Write a Draft Look over the Word Bank chart you made from page 87. Use it to help you write your draft in your notebook. Remember to use specific details.

Revise

Rhyme Authors find the best rhymes by trying different words. Sometimes they have to change an idea several times. Read lines from poems below. Then revise the lines to include pairs of rhyming words.

There was a purple butterfly

that fluttered in the _____.

My dog likes to have fun.

He always tries to _____.

Revise It's time to revise your draft. Read the draft and work on making the words rhyme.

Digital Tools

To learn how to hear your rhyming poem read aloud, watch "Record Audio." Go to **my.mheducation.com.**

Tech Tip

Some websites can help you find rhyming words. Type in a word and you will see some suggestions. You'll have to make the words fit in your poem.

Revise: Peer Conferences

Review a Draft Listen carefully as a partner reads his or her work aloud. Begin by telling what you liked about the draft. Make suggestions that you think will make the writing stronger.

Partner Feedback Write one of your partner's suggestions that you will use in the revision of your poem.

Based on my partner's feedback, I will _____

_____

_____

After you finish giving each other feedback, reflect on the peer conference. What was helpful? What might you do differently next time?

_____

_____

Revision Use the Revising Checklist to help you figure out what text you may need to move, add to, or delete. Remember to use the rubric on page 93 to help you with your revision.

Remember to use the rubric on page 93 to help you with your revision.

Quick Tip

Use these sentence starters to discuss your partner's work.

I was interested in the animal because...

I enjoyed this part of your poem because...

I have a question about...

✓ Revising Checklist

☐ Does my poem fit my purpose and audience?

☐ Does it include rhyming words that relate to the animal?

☐ Did I use details?

☐ Did I use exact words to express my ideas?

Edit and Proofread

When you **edit** and **proofread**, you look for and correct mistakes in your writing. Rereading a revised draft several times will help you catch any errors. Use the checklist below to edit your poem.

Grammar Connections

Sometimes one sentence in a poem is written on two lines. Make sure you use correct punctuation to help a reader understand your poem.

✓ Editing Checklist

☐ Did I use correct punctuation?

☐ Are words spelled correctly?

☐ Are apostrophes used correctly?

☐ Are possessive nouns used correctly?

List two mistakes you found as you proofread your poem.

1 _____

_____

_____

2 _____

_____

_____

Publish, Present, and Evaluate

Publishing Create a clean, neat final copy of your rhyming poem. As you write your final draft be sure to print neatly and legibly.

Presentation Practice reading your poem when you are ready to present your work. Use the Presenting Checklist to help you.

Evaluate After you publish and present your rhyming poem, use the rubric on the next page to evaluate it.

1 What did you do successfully? _____

_____

_____

2 What needs more work? _____

_____

_____

✓ Presenting Checklist

- ☐ Stand up straight.
- ☐ Look at the audience.
- ☐ Read your poem with expression and feeling.
- ☐ Speak loudly so that everyone can hear you.
- ☐ Answer questions using details from your poem.

Listening When you listen actively, you pay close attention to what you hear. When you listen to other students' presentations, take notes to help you better understand their ideas.

What I learned from ....'s presentation:

_____

Questions I have about ....'s presentation:

_____

4	3	2	1
• has many details about an animal	• has some details about an animal	• is about an animal but lacks details	• does not focus on the topic
• includes four or more rhyming words	• includes some rhyming words	• makes an effort to include rhyming words	• lacks rhyming words
• includes precise language	• includes some precise language	• makes an effort to use precise language	• does not include precise language
• is free or almost free of errors	• has few errors	• has errors that distract from the meaning of the poem	• has many errors that make the poem hard to understand

Spiral Review

You have learned new skills and strategies in Unit 2 that will help you to read and understand texts. Now it is time to practice what you have learned.

- Homographs
- Antonyms
- Suffixes
- Main Topic and Key Details
- Problem and Solution
- Beginning, Middle, End
- Diagrams and Labels

Connect to Content

- Pet Owner Book
- Habitat Poster
- Reading Digitally

Read the selection and choose the best answer to each question.

Monarch Butterflies on the Move

1. Would you be able to find the place where your great-grandparents lived? Would you be able to find the place without looking at a map or knowing the name of the place?

2. Monarch butterflies do this. The butterflies travel to the same places, even though they have never been there! In the <u>fall</u>, they migrate, or move, south where older generations once migrated.

3. Monarchs west of the Rocky Mountains fly to California. Monarchs east of the Rocky Mountains fly to the mountains of Mexico. The trip to Mexico is long. They might fly 2,500 to 3,000 miles!

4 When the monarchs finally get to the mountains, they gather on tall trees. The trees keep the air cool and moist. They also offer protection from wind, rain, and snow. The trees are a safe place to rest.

5 In the spring, the days are warmer and longer. Monarch butterflies begin to leave the trees and fly north.

6 The monarchs search for blooming milkweed plants. They lay eggs on these plants. Caterpillars hatch from the eggs. They eat the milkweed plants. Soon, the caterpillars become orange and black butterflies. The children of the monarch butterflies continue the journey back north.

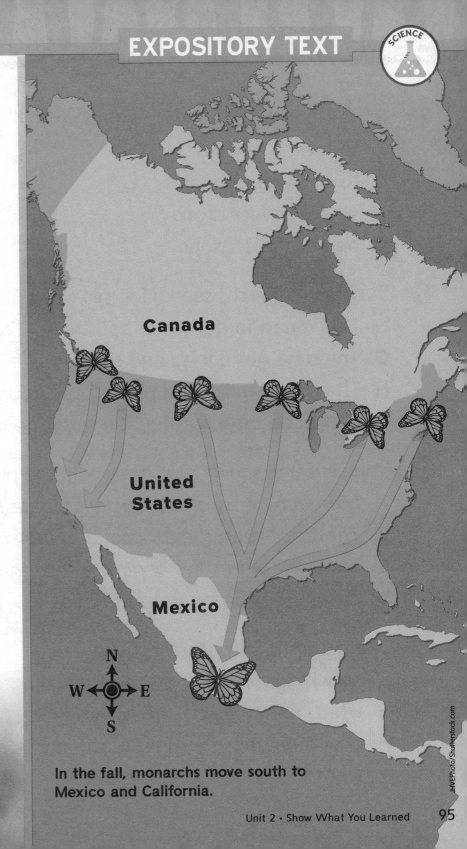

In the fall, monarchs move south to Mexico and California.

SHOW WHAT YOU LEARNED

1 In paragraph 2, the word <u>fall</u> means —

A to hit the ground

B to become quieter

C where a river drops

D one of the seasons

2 Why do monarchs search for milkweed plants?

F They need to gather on tall trees.

G The days get cooler and shorter.

H They need milkweed plants to lay their eggs.

J Milkweed offers protection from the wind.

3 Which detail shows how trees help the butterflies?

A *Monarchs west of the Rocky Mountains fly to California.*

B *The trees keep the air cool and moist.*

C *Monarch butterflies begin to leave the trees and fly north.*

D *Caterpillars hatch from the eggs.*

4 The diagram on page 95 shows —

F how monarchs fly north in the spring

G what monarchs do in the winter

H how monarchs fly south in the fall

J what monarchs do in the summer

> **Quick Tip**
>
> The diagram uses pictures and words to explain something about monarch butterfly migration. Think about what the map and the arrows show.

Read the selection and choose the best answer to each question.

The Fox and the Grapes

1   One day, Fox was walking through the woods. She suddenly stopped. A bunch of purple grapes was hanging from a vine. The grape vine was growing on a tree branch high over Fox's head.

2   The <u>beautiful</u> grapes were big and ripe. They were full of juice. They looked as if they would burst open.

3   Fox knew just how wonderful the grapes would taste. She was hungry. She had only had a few worms and ants to eat for breakfast. Fox jumped up to grab the grapes. But her sharp teeth couldn't reach them.

4   Fox walked a few feet away from the tree. Then she ran and jumped as high as she could. Fox was unsuccessful.

5   Over and over, she ran and leaped. Her mouth never touched the grapes. Fox was getting tired. Now she was hungry and thirsty.

6   Finally, Fox sat down. The grapes no longer looked so ripe and juicy. Fox thought to herself, *Why should I work so hard for a bunch of grapes? They are probably sour instead of sweet.*

7   Fox walked off proudly, lifting her nose in the air.

8   **Moral**: Some people pretend not to <u>like</u> something because they cannot have it.

1 What happens in the middle of the story?

A Fox keeps trying to get the grapes.

B Fox decides she doesn't want the grapes.

C Fox sees the grapes hanging from the tree.

D Fox walks off with her nose in the air.

2 In paragraph 2, what does the word <u>beautiful</u> mean?

F Not pretty

G Full of beauty

H Full of berries

J Not many

3 Fox's feelings about the grapes change because –

A the grapes are not ripe enough to eat

B she is no longer hungry

C the grapes do not taste very good

D she cannot reach them

4 Which of these is an antonym for the word <u>like</u> in paragraph 8?

F Ignore

G Choose

H Love

J Dislike

Quick Tip

To help you identify what happens in the beginning, middle, and end of the story, retell the story in your own words. Use the word *first* to tell what happened in the beginning, *then* to tell about the middle, and *finally* to tell about the end.

Focus on Genre

Reread the fable "Wolf! Wolf!" on pages 130–153 of the **Literature Anthology.**

- Compare the illustrations and what the text says about the wolf's garden on pages 130–131 and 146–147. How and why does the garden change?

_____

_____

_____

- What lesson does the boy learn? What lesson does the wolf learn?

_____

_____

_____

Talk about the characteristics of a fable. What makes *Wolf! Wolf!* a fable? Complete the Graphic Organizer on page 101 to show examples of what happens and why it could not happen in real life.

What Happens	Why It Could Not Happen In Real Life
1	1
2	2
3	3

Homographs

Homographs are words that have the same spelling but different meanings. Homographs may or may not sound the same. To tell which homograph to use, think about the meaning of the sentence.

Circle the correct definition for the homograph listed in bold below.

1 Lucy sits at the **second** desk in the classroom.

part of a minute   next to the first

2 A **wave** washed away the sandcastle.

movement of the sea   move your hand to say hi

3 The **lead** broke while I was writing.

to go in front of a group   material inside a pencil

Think of your own homograph or choose one from the box below. On a sheet of paper, write two sentences with different meanings for the homograph.

wind	ring	letter	well	bow

Write a Pet Owner Book

Write a book to help people take care of their cat, dog, rabbit, or other pet. Include the steps you need to take and these tips:

- Tell what the pet should eat and drink.

- Give examples of toys that the pet would like.

- Share information about grooming (baths, brushing teeth, clipping nails).

- Include information about when a pet should go to the veterinarian.

To help you get started, draw a picture and name the pet you are choosing for your book below.

Quick Tip

Use a chart to help you organize your book. Write the headings "Feeding, Playing, Grooming, and Health."

- Choose only the most important information.

- Think about what pet you can best show in a picture.

EXTEND YOUR LEARNING

Habitat Poster

Use print or online resources to create habitat posters that show habitats and the animals that live in each habitat.

- Explore habitats. Choose at least two habitats.
- Find out what animals live in each habitat.
- Learn how each habitat helps the animals meet their needs for food, water, and shelter.
- Find out how each animal moves through the habitat.
- Draw and label each habitat and the animals living there on a poster.

Write two sentences comparing the habitats and the animals that live there.

_____

_____

Quick Tip

Forests, oceans, deserts, ponds, and mountains are types of habitats. A habitat affects how animals move. For example, fish move through the ocean.

With a partner, go back to "Baby Bears" on pages 110–127 of the **Literature Anthology**. Talk about how you would create a habitat poster for the bears described in the text.

Under the Sea

Log on to **my.mheducation.com**. Reread the online article "Under the Sea." Look at the information found in the interactive features. Answer the questions below.

Under the Sea

Scientists count the fish in the deep blue sea.

Time for Kids, "Under the Sea"

- Why did scientists think that animals could not live in the deep sea?

_____

_____

- What new sea species did the scientists discover?

_____

_____

- Look at the Interactive Map of Ocean Life. What sea life lives in the Atlantic Ocean near Canada? Why is it in danger?

_____

_____

_____

Martin Strmiska/Alamy

What Did You Learn?

Use the rubric to evaluate yourself on the skills that you learned in this unit. Circle your scores below.

	excellent	good	fair	needs work
Homographs	4	3	2	1
Antonyms	4	3	2	1
Suffixes	4	3	2	1
Main Topic and Key Details	4	3	2	1
Problem and Solution	4	3	2	1
Beginning, Middle, End	4	3	2	1
Diagrams and Labels	4	3	2	1

What is something you want to get better at?

_____

_____

Text to Self Think about the texts you read in this unit. Tell your partner about a personal connection you made to one of the texts. Use the sentence starter to help you.

I made a connection to ... because ...

Present Your Work

With your partner, plan how you will present your animal information cards to the class. Discuss the sentence starters below and write your answers.

Beetle

An interesting fact I learned is _____

_____

I would like to know more about _____

_____

✓ Presenting Checklist

- ☐ Practice your presentation with your partner in front of a friend.
- ☐ Stand up straight and make eye contact with your audience.
- ☐ Read your cards with expression.
- ☐ Speak clearly and slowly so the class can understand you.